Goat's Adventure

in Alphabet Town

by Janet McDonnell
illustrated by Tom Dunnington

created by Wing Park Publishers

CHILDRENS PRESS ®
CHICAGO

Library of Congress Cataloging-in-Publication Data

McDonnell, Janet, 1962-
    Goat's adventure in Alphabet Town / by Janet McDonnell ;
illustrated by Tom Dunnington.
       p.   cm. — (Read around Alphabet Town)
    Summary: Goat meets "g" words on her adventure in
Alphabet Town. Includes alphabet activities.
    ISBN 0-516-05407-4
    [1. Alphabet—Fiction. 2. Goats—Fiction.] I. Dunnington, Tom,
ill. II. Title. III. Series
PZ7.M478436Go 1992
[E]—dc 20
                                91-20548
                                   CIP
                                   AC

Goat's *Adventure*

in Alphabet Town

You are now entering Alphabet Town,
With houses from "A" to "Z."
I'm going on a "G" adventure today,
So come along with me.

This is the "G" house of Alphabet Town. Goat lives here.

Goat likes "g" things. She has
lots of them.

Most of all, Goat likes gifts.

One day, Goat's mom said, "Your birthday is coming soon."
"Oh, goody," said Goat.

Goat wondered what she would get.
"I hope Grandma gives me those pretty
green gloves,"

she said.

Goat's birthday came at last. Goat was so glad. At last it was time to open the gifts.

Goat's Mom and Dad gave her a

guitar.

Her grandpa gave her a pair of

glasses.

Her grandma gave her the pretty green gloves she wanted.

And Goat's brother gave her some

gumdrops.

Goat gobbled them up right away.

Soon the gifts were all opened.
Now Goat was sad. She wished
there were more gifts to open.

Then Goat saw one of her friends
outside. That gave her an idea.
"I know," she said. "I will have
a party."

"I will invite

Goose

and Grizzly

and all my friends. Then I will get more gifts."

"You are greedy," said Goat's brother.
"I am not," said Goat. "You are a
grouch." And she walked away.

"I must invite my guests today,"
said Goat. "They will want to get
me gifts. I will go to Grizzly's
house first."

But when Goat got there, she was
greeted by a very sad Grizzly.

"What is wrong?" asked Goat.
"Oh, Goat," said Grizzly. "I am so
sad. My pet fish died. Now I have
no pet."

Goat felt bad. She did not like to
see Grizzly so sad.

23

"Wait here," said Goat. "I will be right back." And then she was gone.

When she came back, she gave Grizzly a gift. "This is for you," said Goat.

Grizzly opened the gift. Then he grinned a big grin. "A new

goldfish

for me," said Grizzly.

"Oh, thank you, Goat." And he gave Goat a big hug. Now Goat felt great.

"I do like getting gifts," said Goat.
"But guess what?

"It is even more fun to give gifts
than to get them."

MORE FUN WITH GOAT

What's in a Name?

In my "g" adventure, you read
many "g" words. My name
begins with a "G." Many of my
friends' names begin with "G"
too. Here are a few.

Gary   Graham   Gail   Guido

Glenna   Gloria   Gordon   Gabby

Do you know other names that start with "G"?

Does your name start with "G"?

Goat's Word Hunt

I like to hunt for "g" words. Can you help me find the words on this page that begin with "g"? How many are there? Can you read them?

girl

magazine

penguin

goose

garbage

sack

pig

dog

Can you find any words with "g" in the middle?
Can you find any with "g" at the end?
Can you find a word with no "g"?

Goat's Favorite Things

"G" is my favorite letter. I love "g" things. Can you guess why? You can find some of my favorite "g" things in my house on page 7. How many "g" things can you find there? Can you think of more "g" things?

Now you make up a "g" adventure.